TIME

MANAGING EDITOR Richard Stengel
DESIGN DIRECTOR D.W. Pine
DIRECTOR OF PHOTOGRAPHY Kira Pollack

Earthquake Haiti: Tragedy and Hope

EDITORS Michael Elliott, Jeffrey Kluger and Richard Lacayo
DESIGNER Cynthia Hoffman
PHOTO EDITOR Paul Moakley
ASSISTANT PHOTO EDITOR Leah Latella
REPORTERS Kathleen Adams, Beth Bland, Ioan Grillo, Barbara Maddux, Andrew Marshall, Jay Newton-Small, Tim Padgett, Austin Ramzy, Mark Thompson and Deirdre van Dyk
EDITORIAL PRODUCTION Rick Prue and Lionel P. Vargas
COPY EDITOR Mary Beth Protomastro

TIME INC. HOME ENTERTAINMENT

PUBLISHER Richard Fraiman
GENERAL MANAGER Steven Sandonato
EXECUTIVE DIRECTOR, MARKETING SERVICES Carol Pittard
DIRECTOR, RETAIL & SPECIAL SALES Tom Mifsud
DIRECTOR, NEW PRODUCT DEVELOPMENT Peter Harper
ASSISTANT DIRECTOR, BOOKAZINE MARKETING Laura Adam
ASSISTANT PUBLISHING DIRECTOR, BRAND MARKETING Joy Butts
ASSOCIATE COUNSEL Helen Wan
BOOK PRODUCTION MANAGER Suzanne Janso
DESIGN & PREPRESS MANAGER Anne-Michelle Gallero
ASSOCIATE BRAND MANAGER Michela Wilde

The publisher will contribute $2 from the sale of each hardcover book in retail trade channels and $1 from the sale of each hardcover book in special sales channels to Haitian relief efforts. The publisher will guarantee a minimum total donation of $75,000 from the sale of all editions of this book.

Of this donation, $25,000 will go to the Clinton Bush Haiti Fund, and the balance of the donation will be given to other Haitian relief efforts.

Additionally, we would like to thank the following individuals and organizations for their generous contributions to this book: Associated Press, Landov Photos, Magnum Photos, Shaul Schwarz—Reportage by Getty Images, Symbology Creative, Reuters Pictures, TCM Promotions, Timothy Fadek—Polaris Images and Zetainteractive.

ISBN 10: 1-60320-163-7
ISBN 13: 978-1-60320-163-6
Library of Congress Number: 2010920940

We welcome your comments and suggestions about TIME Books. Please write to us at:
TIME Books, Attention: Book Editors, P.O. Box 11016, Des Moines, IA 50336-1016

If you would like to order any of our hardcover Collector's Edition books, please call us at 1-800-327-6388
(Monday through Friday, 7 a.m.–8 p.m., or Saturday, 7 a.m.–6 p.m. Central Time)

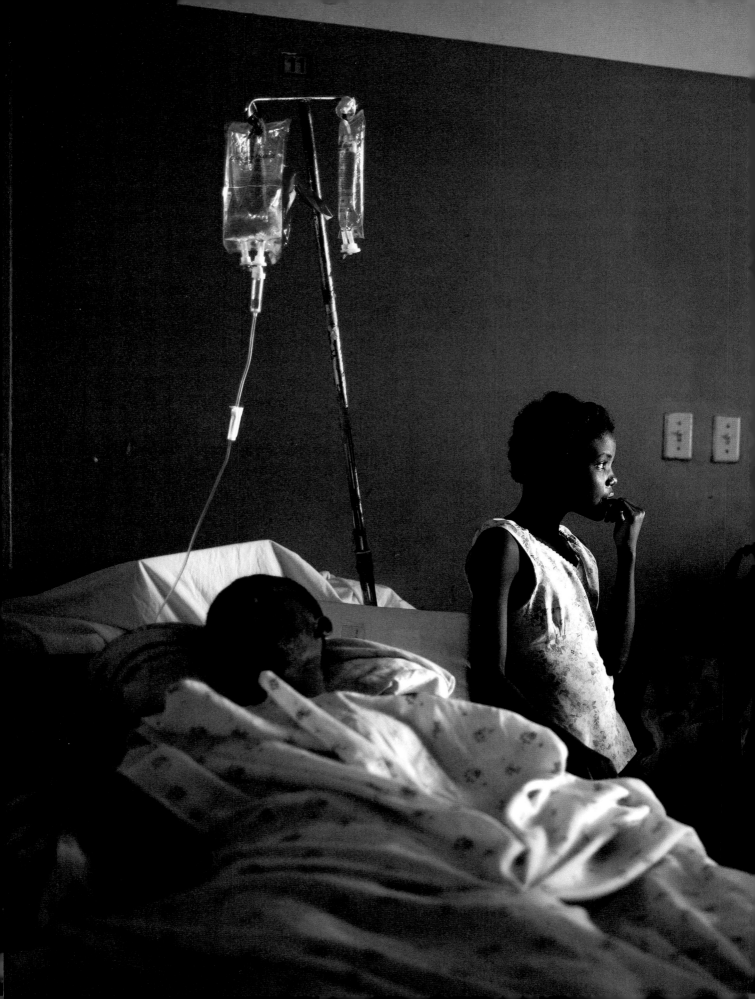

Contents

Dusk till Dawn
Rescue workers rushed to Haiti from around the world— racing against the clock, like this group, to free trapped citizens from the rubble

To Report and Respond

By Richard Stengel
TIME Managing Editor

THE MIND BALKS AT THE SCALE OF LOSS AND DEVASTATION IN HAITI. HOMES REDUCED TO rubble. Legs jutting from a destroyed building. Trucks carrying bloated bodies. The images are disturbing; the words that describe them haunting; the stories wrenching. One wants to turn away. But it is our job as journalists not to.

Stories like that of the earthquake in Haiti and its aftermath cause us to face uncomfortable questions: Do we simply observe and chronicle, or do we try to help, to bring assistance? What is our obligation as journalists, as citizens, as human beings? From the moment our TIME colleagues arrived in Haiti, they faced these same questions, not as if in some journalism class but on the streets. Our reporters and photographers were confronted by Haitian men and women who said, *Put down your cameras. Put down your pens. Do something. Help us.* It is a gut-wrenching challenge. Every reporter knows that inner tug-of-war, that feeling of being caught between being an observer and being an actor in the drama that you're covering. In Haiti, that dilemma was more acute than it usually is—and even at the best of times, it is never one with an easy or simple solution.

For all that, I would say that in the case of Haiti, there is a deep connection between what we have done and have to do as journalists, and the universal desire to help. When we shine a light on a natural disaster like Haiti, we force the world to take notice and foster the will to take action. True, we are not giving immediate aid to those individuals who need it. But our writing and reporting make the case for fixing what is broken, and in doing so, for helping thousands, millions.

The enormous outpouring of both sympathy and dollars after the earthquake came about in part because journalists have focused a remorseless light on Haiti. We have not softened the vision or gilded the story—we have shown the entire palette of emotions and actions, from despair to hope, from heroism to cowardice, from grief to joy, from bravery to craven selfishness. There is a sense of satisfaction in covering a great story, of course, especially if in doing so you can help those who have been hurt, but in the case of Haiti, that did not seem quite enough. That is in part why we have put together this beautiful and moving book, made up of striking images and insightful words. We are donating to Haitian relief $1 for each softback sold and $2 for each trade hardback.

It is only right, and it is not nearly enough, but it is what everyone at TIME wanted to do. Most of us who have worked on the book have not been in Haiti during the tragedy. But we have lived with the images and reports that came from our people there, which helped fuel the idea that we should not just focus attention on the tragedy but help give something back to those who have lost so much. We believe that when something like the Haiti earthquake happens, attention must be paid, and that when it is, help often follows. We are not a charitable organization; we're a journalistic one. But sometimes those things overlap. We cover tragedies, but we do not stand outside the tragedies we cover.

Alive!
More than two days after the quake, a survivor was pulled from the rubble of a collapsed building in Port-au-Prince and carried out on an improvised stretcher

Too Many Bodies
Wearing masks to ward off odor and disease from the unburied and uncountable dead, a group of youngsters runs past the site of a make-shift cremation, one of many

The Desperate Dig
Rescuers had nothing to work with but willing hands as they struggled to find survivors trapped beneath tons of concrete

Frantic

Two women cry in desperation for family members presumed dead under the rubble of a home in Port-au-Prince on Jan. 14. Tens of thousands of the people who died will never be identified

Lost City

By Nancy Gibbs

WE'VE SEEN EARTHQUAKES AND HURRICANES SHRED HOMES, WRECK towns, even rip apart or drown whole cities. But the search for survivors usually does not include the country itself. What is left once the National Palace collapses, and the Parliament, the U.N. headquarters and virtually every government ministry? Once churches have crumbled, and schools and banks; the fanciest hotel in town, and the hospitals, where the dazed and wounded might have found comfort, and the barracks and police stations, where they might have sought safety?

In Haiti, order, safety, comfort, all perished. But the first to die was dignity. There was no time or means to keep her alive once the city of Port-au-Prince was turned inside out, the living tossed from their homes to commune with the dead on the streets. The corpses had to be collected in wheelbarrows and shopping carts; some were consumed on pyres of burning tires. At the city's Grand Cimetière, with its elegant tombs, chickens pecked at the bodies stacked along the central path, left by families who couldn't afford $100 for burial. And those were the lucky ones. Many corpses were loaded by bulldozer into dump trucks and hauled away to mass burials in the cursed swamplands outside the city, where past rulers had buried their enemies. There was not even time to take a picture, seize a chance for certainty. Instead, thousands upon thousands just disappeared one day, and the people who loved them will only

Getting Down to Business
*One week after the quake,
members of the U.S. Army
82nd Airborne touch down
on the grounds of the battered
National Palace*

be able to guess at their grave, in a country that takes the ceremonies of burial so seriously that some families spend more for their crypt than for their home.

To say this could be the worst natural disaster in the modern history of the hemisphere does not begin to tell the story. Nor does the number of dead, named and unnamed, nor the pictures or tweets or accounts of survivors and saviors. Haiti had been a slow-motion disaster for decades, during which billions of dollars in well-intentioned aid vanished with hardly a trace of lasting progress. In such a place, the very idea of rebuilding is hard to fathom. But so is the alternative—the idea that not just people but a country can die.

Is it possible to just start all over?

"We in Haiti thought it was the end of the world."
President René Préval

THE 7.0 QUAKE HIT AT TWILIGHT ON JAN. 12, WITH THE EPICENTER 15 MILES SOUTHWEST of Port-au-Prince. It lasted about 40 seconds; survivors who struggled to keep their cars from pitching off the roads said they could still feel the vibrations in their arms and legs hours later, as if their bones had suffered aftershocks. It was the kind of quake that rings church bells in steeples before they collapse, makes buildings heave and sway like ships at sea, turns stone to powder, wrinkles walls like tissue paper. Seismologists call this a strike-slip earthquake, in which one side of a fault slides horizontally past the other one. The Enriquillo-Plantain Garden fault, underneath Haiti, had slept for 150 years, and scientists had debated whether it would produce a series of small shocks or one big one when it woke. Now they know.

"When the quake hit, it took many seconds to even process what was happening," missionary Troy Livesay reported on his blog. His house began rocking back and forth. "It felt fake. It felt like a movie," Livesay wrote. "Things were crashing all over the house. I do not know why my house stands and my children all lie sleeping in their beds right now. It defies logic, and my babies were spared while thousands of others were not."

As the shocks came in waves, a vast gray cloud of evaporated plaster and cement rose into the air. Houses rolled down into ravines or fell on top of one another into piles of rock, some with arms and legs sticking out. The very wreckage seemed to moan, and survivors listened for cries from deep inside the collapsed buildings, then tried to dig out those trapped using nothing more than bare hands wrapped in cloth. The city's Roman Catholic Archbishop was killed when the force of the quake hurled him off the balcony outside his room; the chief of the U.N. mission and scores of other officials died as their headquarters collapsed. The president of the Senate was trapped when the Parliament building crumbled. At one school, rescuers wore holes in their rubber gloves as they pulled out the bodies of teenage girls in their orange uniforms.

Five hours after the quake, people could still hear buildings crumble. Damage to the city's hospitals did not stop the injured from dragging themselves there hoping for some kind of help—even though countless doctors and nurses had themselves perished. Parents carried their limp children, limbs twisted or crushed, pleading for someone, anyone, to save them. The three Doctors Without Borders facilities were severely damaged or destroyed; the best they could offer, a spokesman said, was "first-aid care and stabilization. The reality of what we're seeing is severe traumas—head wounds, crushed limbs—severe problems that cannot be dealt with at the level of care we currently have available."

As night fell, fires burned, but everywhere else it was total darkness; people still trapped in the rubble of luxury hotels had only their BlackBerrys for light. More than 30 aftershocks rattled the city through the night, so no shelter seemed safe. People built tent cities in the parks or slept in their cars or hotel driveways. One woman gave birth in a park; nearby, an old woman died. The silence was broken mainly by the sound of people singing their prayers, singing through the rolling tremors, praying for the living and the dead. *"Beni swa leternel,"* they sang. "Blessed be the Lord."

Even the following afternoon, workers at Catholic Relief Services said there was not an ambulance or rescue vehicle in sight; the radio stations played "only wild music." People wandered in every direction, their belongings stuffed in sacks or suitcases and carried on their heads. Neighbors shared what they had, formed impromptu search-and-rescue teams, took in stray children; one woman opened her home and yard to about 200 homeless people. The same miracles and mercies played out in the other devastated towns: Jacmel, Léogâne, Petit Goâve. Haiti is a country where people are not used to being taken care of by the government—often, in fact, it's the reverse. And so they take care of themselves and one another, showing in the serial disasters of the past few years the kind of resilience that soft people in safe countries can scarcely imagine.

"Mother, don't let me die."
An 11-year-old girl trapped in the rubble

LUCK TOOK ON A WHOLE NEW MEANING—LIKE BEING BURIED ALIVE IN A SUPERMARKET, where one girl survived on fruit leather for the four days it took her rescuers to dig her out. Reuters reported that a Canadian was able to send a text message about where he was trapped, and it eventually reached Canadian authorities, who sent rescuers. Improvisation was all that was left after every routine and reflex was broken. "We ripped license plates off cars to use as splints," one doctor said. Billboards turned into makeshift roofs. At the Hotel Villa Creole, the Miami *Herald* reported, furniture was turned into gurneys, and hotel guests with no medical training worked as EMTs. Some field hospitals used vodka to sterilize wounds; others were reduced to performing amputations by hacksaw. And still people sang, and suffered, and prayed.

Not all the improvisation was so noble. As the dust settled, the rumors rose; at any moment, people would suddenly break into a panicked run, having heard that a tsunami was coming. Some rumors were started by thieves eager to scoop up whatever folks had left behind. Each day that passed without relief reaching the sick and the hungry gave license to the lawless. Thousands of prisoners from the damaged jail escaped to join the street gangs and thugs who already controlled certain swaths of the capital. They burned the prison records before leaving, making recapture that much harder. They went door to door with sticks and machetes, breaking, entering and stealing stereos and cell phones as well as food and supplies. Toothpaste was in special demand, for lining the nostrils to keep out the stench of the rotting dead. For every thousand patient and faithful people who were sharing what little they had, it took only a few to turn the scene into a Quentin Tarantino movie.

There was street crime, and there was street justice. The New York *Times* reported on a man caught looting who was driven to a park and, as police watched, was stripped, beaten, thrown on a trash pile and then burned to death. Soon the already overwhelmed doctors were having to deal with gunshot wounds as well as crush injuries and quake trauma.

In the absence of all earthly authority, it was a higher power to which many people turned, convening spontaneous prayer services in churchyards beside piles of stained-glass rubble. At Holy Trinity Episcopal Church, all the murals of Christ's life had been turned to powder, except the image of his baptism. On Sunday, people went to church in face masks and whatever remained of their Sunday best.

The human toll of a natural calamity: for the dead, the indignity of waiting for identification and burial …

When pastors returned to their pulpits, which likely as not was a stump or bench, some were at a loss for words. Do they preach about hope—or from the Book of Job?

The swarm of reporters descending to tell the story faced the same dilemma. In the middle of a cold winter, the scenes of tropical despair seemed a world away. The familiar faces were all there—Anderson Cooper and Katie Couric and Geraldo—but they couldn't force the story into its traditional arc of hope and heroism. The world watched an 11-year-old girl pinned in the rubble as neighbors tried to dig her out with their bare hands. The cameras were there when she was finally freed, and that was supposed to be the end of the story—not the epilogue that she died nonetheless after suffering so long, presumably from the infection that spread through her body from her crushed leg. Her last words, her uncle said, were, "Mother, don't let me die." Even the happy stories had sad endings. Once you're pulled out of the rubble … you're still in Haiti. And for the first days, at least, that could be a death sentence.

"Earthquakes don't kill people. Bad buildings kill them."
John Mutter, seismologist and disaster expert at Columbia University's Earth Institute

A POOR COUNTRY HAS VAST SLUMS, AND THIS IS THE QUAKE'S PERVERSE JUSTICE: IF YOU LIVE in a cardboard shanty held together with spit and straw, your house has less power to kill you. It was the more "modern" homes, if that term applies to a country where the notion of a building code is often merely a bargaining chit, that dissolved in a pile of concrete dust. It was the worst possible message in a nation where fate and poverty preside: don't even try to pull yourself up, or your very ambitions will crush you.

… and for the living, the anguish of the search for missing loved ones

Strong people have better survival chances, but for many Haitians, their resilience is more spiritual than physical. Even before the quake, almost half the population did not have any access to clean drinking water. Malnutrition was rampant; 200,000 people have HIV or AIDS; and just half the children were vaccinated against basic diseases like diphtheria. People were known to die on the operating table because the hospital generator went out—and that was before the earthquake. The average healthy life expectancy in Haiti is 44, annual income $660. Given the lack of antibiotics, clean water and sanitation, the deaths from infection and disease could match those from the disaster itself. In the 1994 Rwanda refugee crisis, cholera took some 45,000 lives in less than three weeks. In Haiti the early estimates of 40,000 to 50,000 dead felt like disaster inflation, but rather than revising downward, officials were soon talking about 200,000 dead, 1.5 million homeless and many more at risk.

Even once police returned to the streets, they had to distinguish between the dangerous and the desperate, who were convinced, not without reason, that they would have to find food and water for themselves. This made the next few days that much more excruciating to watch. So much aid, so much need, so far apart. Gathering the supplies was not the problem; helping has never seemed so easy and so hard at the same time. Text "Haiti" to 90999, press SEND—whoosh, $10 goes to the Red Cross, a million dollars just the first day. Everyone was in motion, as though the machinery of mercy were primed—World Vision gathered blankets, water and other supplies; the Red Cross promised tarps and mosquito nets and cooking gear from a warehouse in Panama—as soon as a means of transport became available. Search-and-rescue teams swarmed in from Chile, China, Iceland, Israel, Turkey, cities across the U.S. Medical schools sent planeloads of doctors and nurses to staff field hospitals. Aid groups set

Heavy Loads
Corpses pile up by the hundreds in the parking lot of the main hospital in Port-au-Prince. Within days of the quake, disposing of the dead became a major problem

Gesturing in disbelief, a man returns to his neighborhood to find the charred remains of the restaurant he owned

up Twitter feeds, charities sent emergency appeals, and the money flowed at an astounding pace: more than $200 million from the U.S. in the first week alone.

But getting help where it was needed was a whole other challenge. Planes full of food and water and medicine circled overhead as people on the ground suffered for lack of them. How do you manage to distribute aid through a decapitated country whose government consists of random ministers with laptops? There was no functioning infrastructure, no phones. Relief agencies couldn't land a plane because the airport had only one runway; if they did land, they couldn't drive anywhere down roads that the World Bank called "abysmal" even before they were blocked by bodies and debris. In the best of times, fewer than 1 million of 9 million Haitians had electricity; the power company went bankrupt in 2008. The U.N., with the most experienced people on the ground, counted more than 200 of their own among the dead and missing a week later. Yet somehow the U.N. World Food Programme was supposed to find a way to hand out 100 million prepared meals in the first month.

Daniel Kedar arrived from Israel with a 30-person team ready to dig people out of the rubble, only to find no command structure on the ground. "We listen to the radio station—without cell phones or a central government source for information, it's the only way to find out where to go to search," Kedar said as a Russian team worked behind him to free two men trapped beneath a house in the Delmas neighborhood. "People could have been saved; there were a lot of air pockets in buildings, but people have just written them off. It's adding to the disaster."

The more desperate that people became, the more dangerous it was to help them. When U.N. officials tried to distribute food at the National Palace, the crowds got out of control. Helicopters swarmed like immense insects, dropping off bandages and Gatorade in open fields, then wheeling off again, trying to keep the rotors from stirring up all the dangerous debris or blowing the make-shift roofs off the tents in the sprawling refugee camps. Eventually, with the port still unusable and the airport clogged, U.S. cargo planes began air-dropping pallets of bottled water with parachutes into open fields.

"We're not taking over Haiti."
State Department spokesman P.J. Crowley

THE U.S. DISPATCHED AN ARMADA OF SHIPS, INCLUDING ONE OF THE WORLD'S BIGGEST, the aircraft carrier U.S.S. *Carl Vinson* and the hospital ship U.S.N.S. *Comfort.* The *Vinson* used its 19 helicopters to airlift humanitarian supplies and troops, while the *Comfort* provided medical support. Special-ops teams set up shop at the airport to help direct traffic, since the tower was out; aluminum matting was brought in to boost the runway capacity for the planes coming in at a steady clip. Observation aircraft flew slowly over the city, helping map the worst-hit spots. Ten thousand troops were in the country within days. That made it necessary for the State Department to clarify a delicate point. "We're not," insisted spokesman P.J. Crowley, "taking over Haiti."

But other countries protested that the U.S. military had essentially annexed the airport and given its own missions priority, forcing flights like one carrying an inflatable hospital for Doctors Without Borders to divert to the Dominican Republic—five times. The U.S. was about to learn all over again the price of even the appearance of imperialism. "There are 200 flights going in and out every day, which is an incredible amount for a country like Haiti," Jarry Emmanuel of the World Food Programme told the New York *Times.* "But most flights are for the U.S. military. Their priorities are to secure the country. Ours are to feed. We have got to get those priorities in sync."

Without a functioning government and with the U.N. initially stunned by its own losses, however, many Haitians welcomed an American invasion. "We want American soldiers to be swarming all over this place," said Joel Auguste, 33, a barber who was staying in a refugee camp thrown up in the national soccer stadium. "They shouldn't give one dollar of aid to my politicians because they will just steal it. Let the white man come and hand it out." Auguste once lived in the U.S. himself; he even survived Hurricane Katrina and argues that the appalling U.S. response to that catastrophe is a role model compared with the Haitian government's collapse. "Here it is every man for himself."

Secretary of State Hillary Clinton arrived in Port-au-Prince, met with President Préval and promised that the U.S. "will be here today, tomorrow and for the time ahead." Her husband and his successor as President met at the White House with President Barack Obama, the trifecta of presidential firepower, to raise money and ensure that it is well spent. "What this situation is giving us is an opportunity to build better," said World Bank spokesman Alejandro Cedeño. And that will ultimately be the test; Haitians have shown themselves capable of enormous personal strength in the face of unimaginable suffering. The question now is whether they can create a strong nation, an honest one, that will take not only the assistance the world is waiting to offer—but the responsibility for using it properly as well.

Portfolio

Photographs by Timothy Fadek and Shaul Schwarz

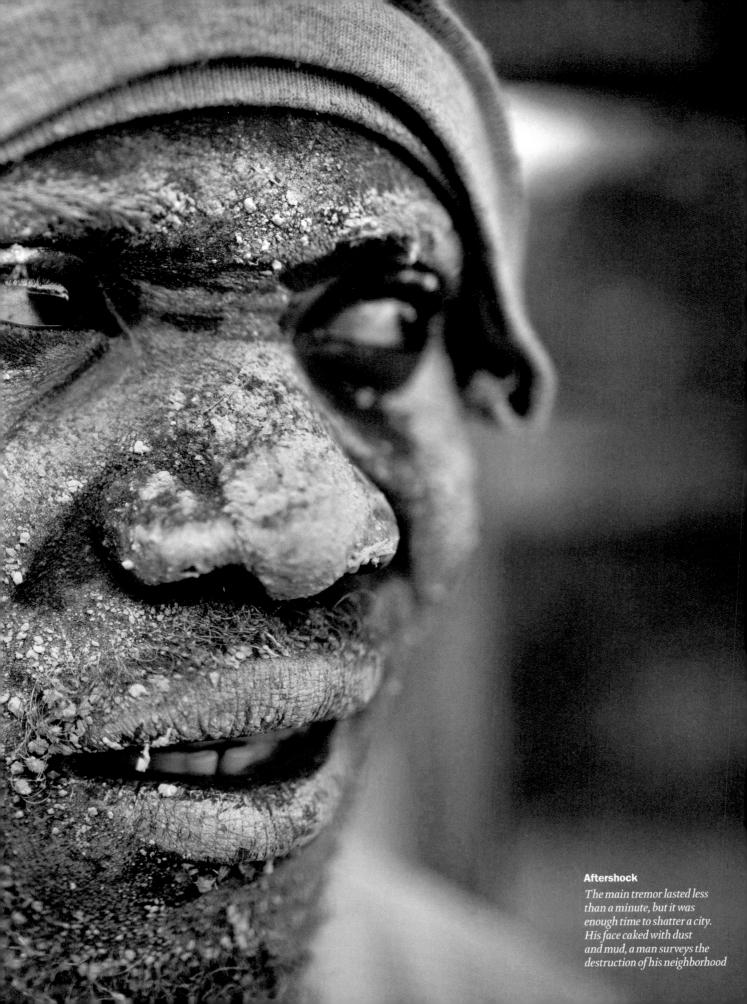

Aftershock

The main tremor lasted less than a minute, but it was enough time to shatter a city. His face caked with dust and mud, a man surveys the destruction of his neighborhood

Bare Ruined Choirs

Helicopters fly above the wreckage of the National Cathedral. The quake brought down the roof, filling the nave with rubble and shattering its stained-glass windows

**Recollections by
Photographer Timothy Fadek**

"I arrived in Port-au-Prince
around 4 o'clock the day
after the earthquake. I
know Haiti—I covered
the civil uprising in
2004—but I was stunned
when I saw the collapsed
presidential palace and
there on the grounds the
beginnings of a huge,
impromptu displacement
camp. There were thou-
sands of people—a sea of
people—sitting on the
grass, shoulder to shoulder,
practically on top of each
other. No one was smiling,
and it was quiet except
for the murmur of people
talking in soft voices.

"The air was very dusty
and extremely humid. The
dust from the debris mixed
with the damp air and
stuck to you. Everywhere
you looked, there was an
inch-thick layer of dust.
And everywhere there
were bodies, trapped in the
rubble, piled in the street,
lined up on the sidewalk.
Some were covered in
white sheets.

"As I walked around and
looked at people, I could
see the shock in their faces.
When I went up to people
to photograph them, they
looked past me blankly.
They were in their own
world. Nobody objected
to my taking their
picture. No one reacted
to me at all."

Death Without Dignity

A bulldozer deposits corpses in a dump truck for burial in mass graves outside the city. The bodies were among hundreds that lay piled for days in the parking lot of the city's central hospital

An Underground Spring
The quake left the city without running water. The bottled variety was scarce and expensive. Here a man collects water from a pool below street level that was created by a broken main

Keeping Faith
Survivors attend Sunday morning Mass outside the badly damaged National Cathedral. Archbishop Joseph Serge Miot was killed when the quake hit the church

Healing Touch
In the hills above the city, an injured woman is treated outside the Villa Creole hotel, where hundreds gathered looking for help. Behind her, others pray and thank God for their lives

SOYBEAN OIL
fortified with
Vitamin A and D
WFP
World Food
Programme
PRODUIT EN HAITI

Food Assistance

In the coastal city of Léogâne, the epicenter of the quake, ACTED, a relief agency based in Paris, helps distribute rice, beans, sugar and cooking oil to hungry survivors

Free-for-All
Early Sunday morning in downtown Port-au-Prince, young men swarm a store, disappearing quickly with kitchenware and whatever else they can carry. Those who linger risk getting their prize nabbed by other looters

Heavy Price

Five days after the quake, in Port-au-Prince's downtown business district, a looter shot by police lies dead in the street while all around him the looting spree continues

**Recollections by
Photographer Shaul Schwarz**

"Yes, there is anger and there is looting, but there is also unity. People are fighting, but I also saw someone take their bottle of water and share it with three others. Those moments are hard to capture in still photography. One of the most touching scenes I saw was about 50 hours after the quake: a group, maybe 10 to 15 people, working together to free a man. They weren't a professional rescue team, just people who had gathered. The wife was standing there, her husband texting her from inside, and the men were trading off working on the problem. I remember thinking, 'There's no way, no way they can do this.' It was a three- or four-story building, and it was just completely devastated. Completely.

"They were climbing through what was the roof. I stood there for a couple of hours, hearing the voices and the knocks. Random people kept stopping in the street and looking and talking it over and putting their neck on the line for someone, when God knows what they've just lost themselves. When they got him out, at least 100 people were gathered. And it was getting dark. And it was quiet. When they carried him out finally, no one cheered. It was a strong moment."

On Guard
Police patrol the shopping district, on the lookout for looters. Days after the quake, the hungry scavenged for food while others snatched goods from unsecured shops

Grim Surplus
Pallbearers carry a coffin into an overflowing Port-au-Prince cemetery. In their haste to bury the dead, some mourners broke into their family mausoleums with hammers

In the Land Of Memory

By Amy Wilentz

WHEN I WENT DOWN TO Haiti for the first time in 1986, it was for no good reason. It's true I had a sneaking suspicion that there was a political crisis there, that the dictator-President Baby Doc Duvalier was being forced out of power. But at the time, I was not a news rat. I'd read Graham Greene's dark novel *The Comedians,* about a hotelier in Haiti under the rule of Duvalier's brutal father Papa Doc, and it painted a picture of a country both alluring and disturbing—and conveniently nearby! I wanted to see the Tontons Macoute, the Duvaliers' silent secret police, in their blue jeans, floppy hats and sunglasses, wielding their waistband pistols and billy clubs. I wanted to see chubby Baby Doc and his skinny-scary wife Michèle Bennett. I spoke French, but otherwise I was very green as a foreign correspondent. I was both innocent and romantic, and that's probably why I had the nerve to go there.

So I flew into François Duvalier International Airport and got into town just a week before Baby Doc fell. I stayed at the legendary Hotel Oloffson; the international media trickled in and then descended en masse. We were all there at the airport in the middle of the night, fighting off the biting red ants and waiting for the moment when Baby

Bearing Any Burden
Haiti seems almost bucolic in this picture of a Sunday market day in 1957, the year Papa Doc began his long, disastrous rule

Baby Doc Duvalier, flanked by his sisters, pays fitful attention during a ceremony in 1969

Doc would leave. And here he came, at the wheel of the family BMW, with his wife, kids, mother, some staff and a lot of money in tow. Michèle looked out from the passenger window of the silver BMW, puffing on a cigarette, bored by the huge crowd of camera-carrying journalists. They drove the car onto an American C-141 Starlifter cargo plane that took off for Paris, and that was it. Bye-bye, Baby. A new era was supposed to begin.

The morning after, Haitians went into the streets by the tens of thousands, uncorked after years of oppression. In front of the blazing white National Palace, they were ecstatic and waved green branches overhead. Hardened foreign correspondents—cowboys who drank barrels of hard liquor and smoked Gauloises—wept uncontrollably in the streets. The Tontons Macoutes fled for their lives, not all successfully.

It was an unforgettable moment, and those of us who covered it were hooked. Even today we Haiti watchers are like a band of brothers and sisters.

But while it has had its precious rewards, following Haiti over the past quarter-century has also been an exercise in impotence, like watching a car speeding toward detritus on a highway while you're at the window of a skyscraper 20 floors above. The car skids over the obstacle and crashes into the median and begins to burn, and you're up there sipping Perrier in your yoga clothes and thinking you should call 911.

THE ROOTS OF THE POLITICAL UNREST AND poverty that have distinguished Haiti go deep into the country's past. The nation has an impressive, even shocking history and certainly a singular one. In the 17th and 18th centuries, thousands of slaves were taken from Africa to this New World island, and from their labor France created a fabulously wealthy sugar-plantation economy. Saint-Domingue, as Haiti was called until 1804, was known informally as the Pearl of the Antilles and was the richest of the French colonies. By the late

Students celebrate Baby Doc's exile on Feb. 7, 1986, by waving branches and torn uniforms of the Tontons Macoute

18th century, there were 500,000 to 700,000 slaves working on plantations, outnumbering the master class at least 10 to 1. When the slave revolt against French rule broke out in 1791, it was not a fair match. No number of Napoleon's soldiers—who fell left and right to yellow fever when they were not killed by rebellious slaves—could put down the revolution. *Koupe tet, boule kay!* was the slaves' war cry: "Cut off heads and burn down houses!" The uprising was bloody and protracted, and it wasn't until 1804 that the Haitians were able to declare their independence from France. It was the only successful slave revolt in the history of mankind.

So it certainly was a remarkable victory: historic, modern in the way the American Revolution was modern. Still, imagine what it meant in regional terms at the time. In 1804 the U.S. was less than 30 years old. A nation that permitted slavery, it now found itself face to face with a free black republic only a nautical dropkick away. The angry war cry

of the slave uprising rang in the ears of American slaveholders. Under Thomas Jefferson, the U.S. refused to recognize Haiti and indeed tried to isolate it as much as possible. It simply was not reasonable or wise to normalize relations with a black republic when nearly all your own people of African descent were enslaved. The U.S. did not recognize Haiti until 1862, after the secession of its own slave states.

The French naturally were also slow to recognize the new nation, and when they offered to do so, it was at a cost: they demanded from the Haitians 150 million francs in gold (which in 1838 was reduced to 90 million francs). They argued that Haiti owed this sum to France as reparations for property the French lost during the revolt. By *property,* the French meant not only plantation lands and houses but also plantation slaves. The Haitians were, in other words, to pay France for their own already hard-won freedom. And pay they did, because otherwise they would have remained under the crippling economic embargo that France, the U.S. and Britain had imposed against the new republic. Paying the debt required Haiti to take out high-interest loans. According to one estimate, at the beginning of the 20th century, Haiti was devoting about 80% of its budget to debt repayment. The entire thing was not paid off until … 1947.

Shouldering a grievous debt burden is not good for getting a fledgling economy up and going. Many observers argue that this obligation was the key element leading to Haiti's culture of poverty. Haiti is still paying off disastrous burdens of debt to the International Monetary Fund, which in light of the quake should now be forgiven.

EVEN WITH HISTORY TAKEN INTO ACCOUNT, there has always been a lot of back and forth among outsiders and among Haitians about why the country remains so troubled and poor. Sometimes people blame the Haitians' traditional African religious practices, also known as voodoo. (Though many Haitians are Catholic or Protestant, many also believe in the old gods. There is a saying about Haiti: 80% Catholic, 20% Protestant, 100% voodoo.) Sometimes they point to centuries of economic dependence, sometimes to the legacy of slavery. There's a bit of truth in each speculation.

I remember my first real voodoo ceremony. It was in a little village called Duverger, on a very still, hot night. I was with a friend who knew the place well; he knew Lucy, Yvette, Bernier, Abner, Adeline, Miss and the twins. He knew the whole town. He'd brought fluorescent flashlights to light up the makeshift peristyle. It was very late, but all the children were up, playing, hanging out, waiting for things to start. The ceremony was big-time entertainment in a place without televisions or movies. The voodoo priest was drinking rum and holding on to the pole at the center of the area where the ceremony was to take place. He poured rum on the ground for the gods; it helps lure them down the pole. And down they came: Erzulie, a flirtatious love goddess, and St. Jacques, the warrior, and Baron Samedi, lord of the cemetery, a favorite of Papa Doc's. Baron always talked in a high-pitched, slightly effeminate whisper that sounded like Papa Doc, and I've often wondered which came first, who was imitating whom.

It's an amateur actor's dream of a religion. When the gods come down, they manifest themselves by possessing one of the congregants. For each god, there are costumes, colors and a special style of speaking. (This is one reason Greene called his novel *The Comedians,* for the word's French meaning, "the actors.") The gods empower the people they've possessed. Baron gives orders, Erzulie arranges relationships, St. Jacques bosses and frightens and metes out justice. I don't remember the particular outcome of that service, but bad romances were fixed, someone agreed to give someone else a few more meters of land, a kid came in to have the priest cure his cold. There was dancing and drumming. We drank the sweetest, strongest coffee to keep us awake.

Obviously voodoo is more than acting and more than dancing and drinking. These gods are archetypes, and they dwell in the Haitian imagination alongside Jesus and Mary. Very few Haitians don't know this religion, and I have heard the best-educated among them blame magic for some event, usually something personal like an accident—in the same kind of superstitious way I might say it rained because I forgot my umbrella. Magical thinking, as Joan Didion would have it.

But when foreign commentators say voodoo sends the message that life is capricious and planning is futile, they are just wrong. Voodoo values life and the interconnectedness of the community. In fact, it's not voodoo but poverty that sends that bad message, the message that life is capricious and planning is futile. Poverty tells you that AIDS and tuberculosis and dozens of other diseases are untreatable, even when the rest of the world has treatments and cures.

Poverty also teaches you to cut down trees. Haiti is badly deforested. Now, of course Haitians don't want to cut down their trees. They're not stupid or backward, as some commentators seem to want to argue. Besides giving fruit and shade, the tree is the symbol of Papa Legba, lord of the universe. Nonetheless, trees have been disappearing at a

Baptism by Fire

In 1956, Haitian women perform a voodoo ceremony in which a child is swung over the flames but comes away from the ordeal unscathed

A gathering in Plaine-du-Nord, on the Atlantic coast, in 1988, a year when Haiti suffered yet another military coup

rapid rate. Why? Because Haitians can no longer eke out enough from the land to feed their families, and a cut-down tree that's been transformed into charcoal can be sold to a market lady from Port-au-Prince for cash, and that cash can be used to buy food and other necessities in the (relatively) new cash economy.

The roots of the countryside poverty are complicated. One reason farming is poor is that Haitians are still using Colonial-era planting and harvesting methods—hoes, scythes—and the farms are small, scattershot family plots. Another reason is that subsidized produce from the U.S. and other nations has been dumped into the Haitian markets for decades, undercutting the price that Haitian-grown stuff can demand in the marketplace and providing a disincentive to cultivators. As the land gave less and less, more and more villagers left their hometowns for Port-au-Prince to find jobs (or, more commonly, not find them) and seek some means of survival.

WHEN I FIRST WENT TO PORT-AU-PRINCE IN 1986, it was a sleepy little city of about 800,000 people, surrounded by small farms and a few villages. Bougainvillea tumbled down flaking walls that hid tangled gardens. Gingerbread houses lined a few of the nicer streets. There were two big slums: Cité Soleil, on the way to the airport, and La Saline, nearer downtown. There was a nightclub on the waterfront where Haitian couples danced merengue in fancy clothes until almost dawn. Uptown there were superluxurious restaurants that invariably served pâté de foie gras. But otherwise the whole city seemed to me a chaotic jumble of color and cement, of electrical wires and sidewalk markets and piles and piles of goods made in China. I was new to Port-au-Prince. After I went down to live there and write a book, I began to grow more accustomed to its rhythms and sights.

After a while, I stopped noticing the brightly colored minibuses. I was no longer surprised when I saw a truck delivering water to the slums and leaking giant puddles, or pigs rooting about in sewage near the port. I ceased to be so paralyzed by the poverty and began to see instead the indomitable industry of the Haitians. I had never anywhere seen people who were busier. Of course, they had to be busy: just to get water, you often had to have a plan that required at least half a day and a walk of a mile or more. As one friend said, laughing, "Yeah, sure we're busy. But we never get anything done!"

Haitians are always laughing. You have to develop a major ironic sense of humor when you live in such hard conditions. In particular, Haitians enjoy a good laugh at the expense of foreigners who say nice things about Haiti. I remember once telling a Haitian friend that I loved his country. "If you love it so much," he said, "what about this plan? You give me your passport, and you stay here while I go to your place."

But when I visited last year, I realized the Port-au-Prince of my first days there was no longer a medium-size town. This city of almost 2 million now stretched out over the nearby farmland and farther. The green outlying area of La Plaine, where the future President Jean-Bertrand Aristide started building himself a huge house in the late 1980s, was now just another Port-au-Prince neighborhood, as was Freres, another village, which used to seem to me about a day's drive away through the country. And up and down the steep ravines that line the roads from Port-au-Prince to the wealthy suburb of Petionville up the hill were new shantytowns seemingly made of plaster and glue and paper clips and washboards and oil drums and pieces of cardboard and tin, where the new people from the countryside were living. You couldn't see any life there from a distance, because the houses were built so close to one another, both horizontally and vertically, that the roofs blocked the sight lines.

All that is gone now, in rubble at the bottom of the ravines.

WHEN A CITY IS LEVELED, AS WITH NEW Orleans or Hiroshima, you have so many memories of it and so many connections, now severed, that it's as if you'd lived a fiction, a novel, instead of your real life. (Haiti has something of a fictional quality on the best of days anyway.) For me, it now seems as if every moment I spent there—having ginger tea with a friend, chatting with a blue-eyed priest as gunfire rang out in the city below, going to an exuberant funeral, watching Aristide rearrange his eyeglasses and give a speech, sitting at a car wash as orphan boys used rags to somehow get my car dirtier—was nothing more than a prelude to the quake. Many of my friends have survived, but some have not been heard from. I'm ready to mourn them and the 100,000 or more who died. But I've shed only a few tears so far, I think because I'm still in shock. I'm not in Haiti yet, so I don't viscerally believe it. A friend of mine has written that even now, after pulling friends, dead, out of the rubble with his hands, he can't believe or understand all he has lost.

And, of course, even what is lost is not entirely lost. You lose the palace, but not the memory of the palace; you lose the child, the mother, the grandparents, the husband, but not the memory of those people. Over time, memories come to replace the people and places, inadequately, but nonetheless. Parents pass down the memory to children, or aunts to nephews, or friends to friends' children, and on through generations. Books guard and concentrate those memories, and art does too, and photographs, scattered throughout the world. In Managua, another city that suffered a terrible earthquake, people still give memory directions: take me past the square where the old oak tree used to be, then go left at the corner where that church was. Reality is fleeting, and what seems substantial is not really so. We know this in some way every day as we walk around doing laundry and driving to work and picking up kids. We know that life is precious, and every minute valuable. But nothing can ever bring this understanding of life's ephemeral quality home so quickly, so solidly and so absolutely as this utter destruction, wrought in less than a minute's time.

Wilentz is the author of The Rainy Season: Haiti Since Duvalier *and other books. She teaches journalism at the University of California at Irvine*

The Long Wait
Seemingly endless lines for food and water tested the patience—and the strength—of Haiti's survivors

Picking Up The Pieces

By Bryan Walsh

THE SUDDENNESS—THAT'S WHAT SETS AN EARTHQUAKE APART FROM STORMS, floods or any other disaster we call an act of God. One moment a city stands, and as little as a minute later, all is rubble. Port-au-Prince tumbled in just that way on the evening of Jan. 12, when a 7.0-strength temblor ruptured the Haitian capital. Tens of thousands, perhaps far more, were killed instantly—but more than that, a city and a country were undone. "I've seen the aftermath of hurricanes and landslides, but nothing on the scale of what happened to Port-au-Prince," says Peter Haas, executive director of the Appropriate Infrastructure Development Group, who arrived in Haiti shortly after the quake. "It's mindboggling. Everything is destroyed."

That minute's worth of destruction will take years—or longer—to repair. As rescue work shifted to recovery work, it was soon obvious that a monumental effort from the international community and the shell-shocked Haitian people would be needed to prevent the catastrophe from growing even worse. The physical infrastructure of the capital is shattered. The public health system, such as it was, is obliterated, and what's left will struggle to cope with tens of thousands of badly injured survivors and the diseases that spread among people who have become refugees in their own country. The government is crippled and all but invisible. The country's nascent economic recovery—its GDP grew 2.3%

Help from Above

Infrastructure in Port-au-Prince was so badly damaged that the U.S. military was forced to airdrop some of its first rounds of aid

in 2008—would surely seem to be the last victim of the catastrophe. "This is really an unprecedented situation," says U.N. Secretary-General Ban Ki-moon—and he feels it personally. The U.N. counted more than 200 of its own people among the dead and missing in the quake, the worst disaster the global body has suffered in its 65-year history. "It is overwhelming for the [Haitian] government, the international community, everyone."

Putting the broken country back together will be hard enough. But Haiti, the poorest country in the western hemisphere, can't and shouldn't simply be restored to what it was before the quake. The catastrophic death toll was a result not so much of the earthquake's strength but of Haiti's history of corruption, its shoddy buildings and ultimately its poverty. As we've seen in the aftermath of previous disasters—including the 2004 Asian tsunami and Hurricane Katrina—rebuilding takes time, commitment and sustained funding, but it can pay off. In the Indonesian province of Aceh, a multibillion-dollar international recovery effort has built more than 100,000 homes—and helped quell a long-running civil war that seemed every bit as intractable as Haiti's entrenched poverty. In the Chinese province of Sichuan, where a quake killed nearly 90,000 in May 2008, the rebuilding process is moving ahead at astounding speed. What was destroyed can be restored—and improved. "You can build and reconstruct a more resilient community," says Dennis Mileti, author of *Disasters by Design.*

In the case of Haiti, that work is vital for both the country and the larger world. The planet's population is set to expand past 9 billion by midcentury—and nearly all that growth will be in cities in the developing world, like Port-au-Prince. More and more people will be living in the danger zone for earthquakes, storms and floods. Unless we prepare the poorest societies for disaster, we'll be chasing worsening crises for decades. "It would be unconscionable to turn Port-au-Prince back to the way it was," says John Mutter, a seismologist at Columbia University. "You have to use this as a perverse chance to build back better."

WHEN A COUNTRY HAS BEEN AS BADLY HURT AS HAITI, WHAT IT NEEDS FIRST IS A HELPING hand from the rest of the world—and Haiti got that. Americans gave at a rate on track with record-setting donations after the tsunami and Hurricane Katrina, and countries as impoverished as the Democratic Republic of Congo and Rwanda sent money. But that eagerness to help was stymied at first by a logistical nightmare. Port-au-Prince's seaport was rendered unusable, its airport was barely functional, and its roads were snarled by debris, the homeless and even the dead. Not only did the quake strike a country mired in poverty; it erupted just 15 miles (about 24 km) from that nation's capital. The government of Haiti was essentially missing in action, leaving a vacuum of authority. Aid and personnel initially had to be shipped in, through either the neighboring Dominican Republic or secondary airports in Haiti. But challenging as the quake's aftermath proved for the U.N. and the NGOs desperate to get aid and medical assistance through, for the locals it was far worse. With Port-au-Prince gone, there was no Plan B, nowhere they could escape to. "With Katrina, if you could walk to the edge of a disaster area, you could get in a car, drive 40 miles, find a store and buy what you needed," says Caryl Stern, president and CEO of the U.S. fund for UNICEF. "Here there is no car. There is no highway. There is no 40 miles away."

In the midst of that desperation, with the very symbols of law and order in ruins, it might not have been surprising if Haiti had reacted in violence. And indeed, there were isolated cases of looting, and crowds could become unruly when it became clear there was too little aid for far too much need. Yet Haiti did not explode. Instead, the people did what others have done after natural disasters throughout the world: they improvised, helping one another while they hoped for aid. It helped that after years of political instability, Haiti had turned a corner, and hope had been spreading on the streets. "There was more goodwill there on the eve of the earthquake than the country had seen in

As survivors called out for help, there were too many hungry people and never enough provisions to feed them all

decades," says Jocelyn McCalla, a Haitian-American development consultant. Haitians "look more poised to come together and roll up our sleeves."

BUT THAT SPIRIT WON'T BE ENOUGH TO REBUILD HAITI IN ANY LASTING WAY. FOR THE short and medium term, international aid will be needed to keep supplies flowing. Water is the first priority; people can go hungry longer than they can go thirsty, and contaminated water can lead to outbreaks of diseases like cholera and diarrhea, especially dangerous for children. Desalination will be one option—the aircraft carrier U.S.S. *Carl Vinson,* holding off the coast of Haiti, can donate 200,000 gal. (about 757,000 L) of fresh water a day. Steady food aid will be necessary for some time—though there are hopes that the earthquake left Haiti's agricultural sector mostly unscathed. The assistance efforts have to be visible, to assure Haitians they haven't been forgotten and to forestall rage on the ground. "We have to give people hope to move away from despair," says Jordan Ryan, assistant administrator for the U.N. Development Programme, which will take the lead on long-term recovery.

There will also be a pressing need for doctors—those who can handle traumatic injuries and those who can provide disease care. But that's just the beginning. Haiti was a sick country before the quake, with a high prevalence of diseases like HIV and tuberculosis that need consistent treatment. Interruption can mean death. Further down the line, Haiti's ruined public-health infrastructure will have to be rebuilt, and that will mean more than just replacing collapsed hospitals. Local talent will be needed, and especially important will be nurses and support staff. Without such a sustained effort, the "long-term ramifications could lead to more deaths than the event itself," says Tom

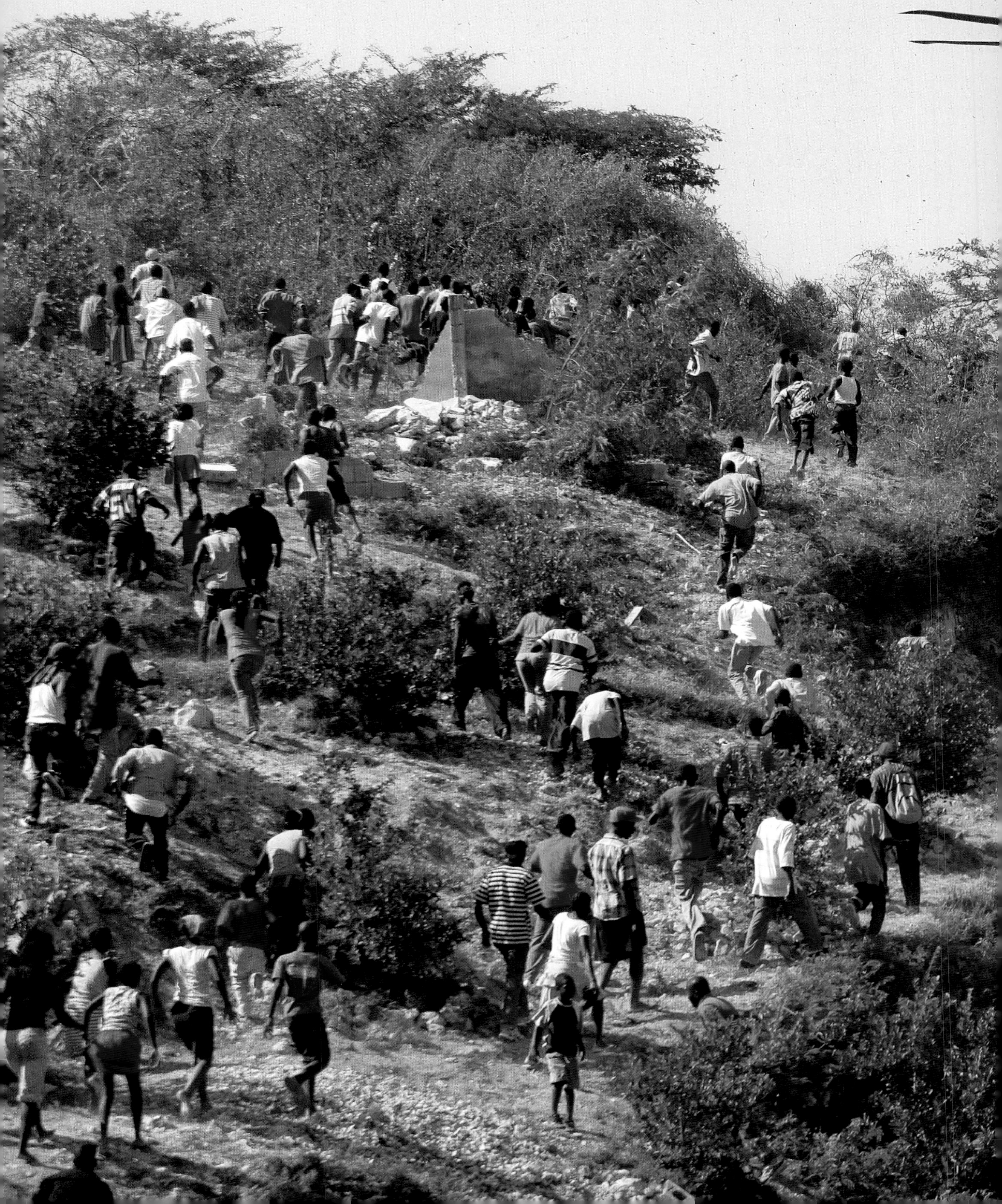

Calling in the Cavalry

In the days after the quake, the U.S. military took the lead in delivering food and water to the struggling survivors in Haiti

The Youngest Survivors

*In a rare moment of levity,
Haitian children played
with empty boxes of food
aid. Nearly half of Haiti's
population is under 18 years old*

City of Survivors
*More than 1.5 million
Haitians were left homeless,
and many were forced to
live in tent cities on the
streets of Port-au-Prince*

Kirsch, a co-director of the Center for Refugee and Disaster Response at Johns Hopkins University.

Perhaps most of all, a recovering Haiti must change the way it builds. The shoddiness of construction in Port-au-Prince made the death toll dramatically higher than it had to be. The 1989 earthquake in the San Francisco Bay Area was of almost the same magnitude as Haiti's earthquake, but it killed only 63 people. A concrete block in Haiti might weigh an eighth of what its U.S. counterpart would, as unscrupulous contractors take their kickbacks and building codes go unenforced. This is corruption that kills—and it's not limited to slums; grand buildings like the presidential palace collapsed too. Other developing countries in quake zones, like Colombia, build far more securely. It may seem as if the last thing Haiti can afford to worry about now is building codes, but dependable homes, hospitals and schools literally mean the difference between life and death. "The quality of the buildings makes a huge difference in the death toll of an earthquake," says Brian Tucker, president of GeoHazards International, which provides consulting services on seismological risk. "And there's no reason that a country like Haiti can't better prepare itself for the next one."

That's exactly why recovery will never be complete unless Haiti can break out of the economic basement. The country has a per capita GDP of $1,300—one-sixth that of the Dominican Republic, with which it shares the island of Hispaniola. Before the quake, Haiti had begun to do better, and in the initial phase of recovery there will be jobs in reconstruction. But consistent aid policies that include microloans for small businesses and more-liberal tariffs that would nurture a low-cost export sector could help Haiti grow sustainably. Even in its present disastrous condition, Haiti has a lot going for it: a great location next to the biggest consumer nation in the world, regional security that sub-Saharan nations would love and a population that has proved resourceful—when given the chance. Long-term reconstruction could give the country that chance, and a richer Haiti would be a safer Haiti. "Part of recovery has to mean charting a new role for Haiti in the global economy," says Ben Wisner, a research fellow at Oberlin College and a disaster expert.

THERE IS PLENTY OF REASON TO BELIEVE THAT THE KIND OF RECOVERY HAITI NEEDS IS possible. More than $10 billion was spent on aid and recovery for nations hit by the Asian tsunami, and though the effort was hardly problem-free—it was marred by corruption, poor coordination and the paradox of too much money chasing too few immediate uses—the Indonesian province of Aceh is back on its feet. In Indonesia the national ministry of public works issued guidelines for reconstruction of more quake-resistant buildings, and the country managed to produce much safer housing for Aceh. Bruno Dercon, an adviser in Indonesia to the U.N.'s housing program, estimates that of the 140,000 houses built after the tsunami, a third are above standard and a third are about standard. "Building back better is not just about engineering codes," he says. It's also about rooting out corruption—and Indonesia, which routinely ranks high on international lists in that unenviable category, has started to do that. There's no reason Haiti can't do the same.

The recovery in Sichuan is even more impressive: just six months after the quake, the homeless were nowhere to be found. Of course, China's strong central government and turbocharged economy helped a lot. But Sichuan province, like Haiti, was a place where graft was common, and so were substandard buildings—which led directly to the quake's staggering death toll. Today, Sichuan is one of the riskier places in China to skim funds, though Beijing's firm hand might be difficult to imitate in blasted Port-au-Prince. "A place like Haiti—that's going to be a struggle," says Ramsey Rayyis, regional representative for the American Red Cross in China. "You're going to need a lot more external intervention."

Another lesson from past disasters is that whenever possible, reconstruction has to be led by the local government—and that might be Haiti's biggest challenge. Although Haitian President René Préval was seen as a significant improvement from a series of controversial leaders like Aristide and

Teams of rescuers from around the world flooded Haiti. They were able to pull some victims from the rubble—but too few

military dictators like François (Papa Doc) Duvalier, Haiti still ranked as the 10th most corrupt country in the world last year, according to the global watchdog Transparency International. And the flow of reconstruction funds will offer ample opportunity for kickbacks and theft—as happened during the tsunami recovery. Yet that can't be an excuse. As successful international NGOs like Partners in Health know, the only sustainable solutions for Haiti are ones implemented by Haitians themselves. "We have to work to build back the capacity of the Haitian government to cope," says the U.N.'s Ryan. "We need to make sure the locals know they have to do the heavy lifting."

So what does the world owe Haiti? Certainly, there is a practical incentive to save the country. Natural disasters—earthquakes, storms, floods—are unavoidable acts of God. But it's possible to build societies, from New Orleans to Port-au-Prince, that can weather them. Doing so would save lives and the tens of billions of dollars spent every time a fragile community gets wiped out. "The world can't afford more of these disasters," says Roger Bilham, a seismologist at the University of Colorado. But there's a moral imperative too. Haiti's dead were victims of poverty and neglect, not just the quake. We have a responsibility to the survivors to help build a Haiti that will never again be so vulnerable.

Beyond All Help
International assistance was even slower to reach remote cities like Léogâne, where Haitians began to rebuild on their own

What Haiti Needs

By Bill Clinton

HILLARY AND I WENT TO HAITI FOR THE FIRST TIME IN DECEMBER 1975. A banker friend of ours had some business down there. He had built up a lot of frequent-flyer miles and called and said he was giving us a delayed honeymoon. We were married in October, and we went down there in December. Both of us just kind of fell in love with the country, and I have kept up with it ever since.

Why is Haiti so special to me? Haiti is completely unique in our hemisphere because of its history and culture. There are other French Caribbean islands, but none of them have Haiti's particular Creole influence. None of them feature Haiti's distinctive mix of West African religious and cultural influences, the most visible of which is the persistence of the voodoo faith, which is practiced alongside Christianity. Unfortunately, ever since the first slave revolt by Haitians in 1791, the country has been beset by abuses caused from within and without. It has never been able to fulfill its potential as a nation.

But I think it can. Haitian immigrants do very well when they come to America or France or Canada. I've always thought that given the right organization and support, Haiti could become a self-sustaining and very successful country. I still believe that.

In order to stave off a disaster and get Haiti on its feet again, the world needs to respond in rapid

Former President Clinton, visiting Port-au-Prince on Jan. 18, 2010, was a whirlwind of activity, surveying the damage, helping

and coordinated fashion. The focus first must be on search and rescue, and on meeting people's basic human needs. After the Oklahoma City bombing in 1995, where just one building was bombed and we had all the help in the world, it still took several days before all the living and dead had been accounted for. There were survivors who were recovered many hours later in the rubble.

We need to get as much equipment as we can into Haiti. The military is sending in helicopters, and there will probably be a need for it to supply some logistics and communications support. The U.S. is going to have to carry a lot of the load there early on. But it's very important that the U.S., which is so pivotal to this emergency period, work very closely with the U.N. peacekeeping mission stationed in Haiti, which is very well organized and is operating well. In fact, the U.N. system has already swung into action: it has offered $10 million in immediate emergency relief and organized food relief through the World Food Programme. There are hundreds of thousands of people who are going to be coming out of there alive who have to be cared for; the World Health Organization is trying to meet the health care needs.

The international relief effort that followed the Asian tsunami of 2004 offers some lessons that can be applied in Haiti. First of all, there has to be national buy-in by the U.S. There has to be a national vision, and I think we have that. Secondly, coordination is really important both within the U.N. and among all the donor countries and nongovernmental groups. There are 10,000 nongovernmental organizations working in Haiti, the highest number per capita in the world except for India. We've got to all work together toward a common goal. We have to relentlessly focus on trying to build a model that will be sustainable, so we don't plant a bunch of trees and then revert to deforestation, or adopt a

unload relief supplies, conferring with the military and giving a press conference at the Port-au-Prince airport

program to bring power to the country that can't be sustained, or adopt an economic strategy that is going to wither away in two years.

I'm trying now to get organized to make sure not only that we get the emergency aid that Haiti needs but also that donors come through on their pre-existing commitments. We need to keep the private sector involved. Once we deal with the immediate crisis, the development plans the world was already pursuing have to be implemented more quickly and on a broader scale. I'm interested in just pressing ahead with it.

Haiti isn't doomed. Let's not forget, the damage from the earthquake is largely concentrated in the Port-au-Prince area. That has meant a tragic loss of life, but it also means there are opportunities to rebuild in other parts of the island. So all the development projects, the agriculture, the reforestation, the tourism, the airport that needs to be built in the northern part of Haiti—everything else should stay on schedule. Then we should simply redouble our efforts once the emergency passes to do the right sort of construction in Port-au-Prince and use it to continue to build back better.

Before this disaster, Haiti had the best chance in my lifetime to fulfill its potential as a country, to basically escape the chains of the past 200 years. I still believe that if we rally around them now and support them in the right way, the Haitian people can reclaim their destiny.

Former President Bill Clinton is the United Nations special envoy for Haiti. He and former President George W. Bush have set up the Clinton Bush Haiti Fund (clintonbushhaitifund.org)

SPECIAL THANKS TO:

Christine Austin, Jeremy Biloon, Glenn Buonocore, Jim Childs, Susan Chodakiewicz, Rose Cirrincione, Jacqueline Fitzgerald, Nina Fleishman, Carrie Frazier, Lauren Hall, Jennifer Jacobs, Brynn Joyce, Ratu Kamlani, Mona Li, Robert Marasco, Amy Migliaccio, Brooke Reger, Dave Rozzelle, Ilene Schreider, Adriana Tierno, Alex Voznesenskiy, Sydney Webber and Jonathan White

Photo Credits

Front cover: Gerald Herbert—AP
Inside cover: Shaul Schwarz—Reportage/Getty Images for TIME
Back cover: Shaul Schwarz—Reportage/Getty Images for TIME

Page 3: Shaul Schwarz—Reportage/Getty Images for TIME **4-5)** Shaul Schwarz—Reportage/Getty Images for TIME **7)** Carlos Barria—Reuters **8-9)** Shaul Schwarz—Reportage/Getty Images for TIME **10-11)** Timothy Fadek—Polaris for TIME **12-13)** Shaul Schwarz—Reportage/Getty Images for TIME **14-15)** Timothy Fadek—Polaris for TIME **17)** Gregory Bull—AP **20-21)** Carolyn Cole—Los Angeles Times/Polaris **22-26)** Timothy Fadek—Polaris for TIME **28-31)** Shaul Schwarz—Reportage/Getty Images for TIME **32-37)** Timothy Fadek—Polaris for TIME **38-41)** Shaul Schwarz—Reportage/Getty Images for TIME **42-43)** Timothy Fadek—Polaris for TIME **44-47)** Shaul Schwarz—Reportage/Getty Images for TIME **48-49)** Timothy Fadek—Polaris for TIME **50-51)** Shaul Schwarz—Reportage/Getty Images for TIME **53)** Herbert List—Magnum Photos **54)** Polaris **55)** Danny Lyon—Magnum Photos **57)** Eve Arnold—Magnum Photos **58)** Bruce Gilden—Magnum Photos **60-61)** Shaul Schwarz—Reportage/Getty Images for TIME **63)** James L. Harper Jr.—U.S. Air Force **65)** Miami Herald/MCT/Landov **66-67)** Jae C. Hong—AP **68-69)** Ariana Cubillos—AP **70-71)** Logan Abassi—The United Nations **73)** Charles Eckert—Atlas Press **74-75)** Timothy Fadek—Polaris for TIME **77)** Jeremy Lock—MIA/Landov **78-79)** from left: Marco Dormino—The United Nations; 2:Lynne Sladky—AP; 2:Olivier Laban Mattei—AFP/Getty Images